W9-BEU-814

ALL ABOUT FOOTBALL

INSIDE COLLEGE FOOTBALL

Preparing for the Pros?

by John Walters

ALL ABOUT FOOTBALL

Inside College Football: Preparing for the Pros?

by John Walters

Mason Crest
450 Parkway Drive, Suite D
Broomall, PA 19008
www.masoncrest.com

Printed and bound in the United States of America.

Series ISBN: 978-1-4222-3576-8
Hardback ISBN: 978-1-4222-3579-9
EBook ISBN: 978-1-4222-8302-8

First printing
1 3 5 7 9 8 6 4 2

Produced by Shoreline Publishing Group LLC
Santa Barbara, California
Editorial Director: James Buckley Jr.
Designer: Bill Madrid
Production: Sandy Gordon
www.shorelinepublishing.com

Cover photograph by Chris Williams/Icon Sportswire/Newscom.

Library of Congress Cataloging-in-Publication Data is on file with the Publisher.

CONTENTS

Key Icons to Look For

Words to Understand: These words with their easy-to-understand definitions will increase the reader's understanding of the text, while building vocabulary skills.

Sidebars: This boxed material within the main text allows readers to build knowledge, gain insights, explore possibilities, and broaden their perspectives by weaving together additional information to provide realistic and holistic perspectives.

Educational Videos: Readers can view videos by scanning our QR codes, providing them with additional educational content to supplement the text. Examples include news coverage, moments in history, speeches, iconic sports moments, and much more!

Text-Dependent Questions: These questions send the reader back to the text for more careful attention to the evidence presented here.

Research Projects: Readers are pointed toward areas of further inquiry connected to each chapter. Suggestions are provided for projects that encourage deeper research and analysis.

Series Glossary of Key Terms: This back-of-the-book glossary contains terminology used throughout this series. Words found here increase the reader's ability to read and comprehend higher-level books and articles in this field.

CHAPTER 1

Early football games were little more than free-for-alls, with few rules and almost no padding or protective gear.

ALL AROUND COLLEGE FOOTBALL

The first college football game took place on the afternoon of November 6, 1869 in New Brunswick, New Jersey. (It could not have taken place at night, since the first practical light bulbs were still a few years away from being invented, actually just a few miles from the site of the game.) A few of the lads from the College of New Jersey, which would later be renamed Princeton University, traveled 17 miles north to take on the Queensmen of Rutgers University. The home team prevailed 6–4, in front of roughly 100 spectators. In a foreshadowing of the deeply rooted passions that would envelop the sport, the visiting team's players were literally run out of town by the Rutgers fans.

Words to Understand

charismatic having a lot of charisma: an ability to charm, inspire, and lead people

distinguishes separates, shows the differences between

governing body an organization or association that works to create rules and structures for a large group of similar organizations (in this case, college athletic departments)

Nearly 150 years later, both Princeton and Rutgers still play football, although the two schools have not played one another since 1980. Since that first game was played, using rugby-style rules, Americans have seen the invention of the telephone, the automobile, the airplane, the television, and the computer. College football was here before all of those creations, and it is more popular today than it has ever been.

Pageantry

The game on the field has all of the same rules as the game that is played on Sundays in the NFL, with a few minor exceptions (e.g., a receiver needs to have only one foot in bounds while making a catch in college football, as opposed to both feet in the NFL).

What most **distinguishes** college football from its professional cousin are the trappings surrounding the games: marching bands, mascots, student-cheering sections, alumni—even boosters.

Whereas the NFL is based in major cities, college football is mostly played in college towns. The NFL exception is Green Bay, Wisconsin, home of the Packers. Their founder, Curly Lambeau, played one season at Notre Dame under the most legendary college football coach of all, Knute Rockne. College football is played in places such as Ann Arbor, Michigan; Tuscaloosa, Alabama; and Stillwater, Oklahoma—towns that the average sports fan might never have heard of, or visited, if it weren't for college football.

In such towns, whose populations might be fewer than 100,000 when you subtract the students, stadiums fill up with more than 100,000 people on football Saturdays. When the University of Nebraska Cornhuskers play a home game at 85,000-seat Memorial Stadium, which has been sold out for 347 consecutive contests dating to 1962, the stadium is larger than all but two cities in the entire state.

The names, such as Cornhuskers, are yet another aspect of college football's charm. Fighting Irish. Crimson Tide. Volunteers. Buckeyes. Sooners. Longhorns. Tar Heels. Colleges simply have better team names than any professional sports teams do.

Purdue University's marching band boasts "The World's Largest Drum." The University of Colorado's football team runs onto the field accompanied by Ralphie, a live buffalo. Outside Tiger Stadium in Baton Rouge, LSU has a compound for its own live tiger, Mike. Before every home game Ohio State's marching band spells out "Ohio" in script, and it is a moment of honor for the band member who is selected to "dot the i."

Such traditions are a product of the sport spanning generations, but also of the intense enthusiasm its fans have for college football. The NFL is a lot like McDonald's: No matter where you travel in this country, the menu remains the same and the structures pretty much resemble one another. College football is a family-owned restaurant. You're in for a surprise, but you're usually in for a treat, as well.

Evolution

That first game in 1869 featured two teams of 25 men with 100 or so spectators. Today, a typical Division I college football program, with players, coaches, staff members, and student volunteers, includes more than 200 people. A few games draw as many as 110,000 fans

(and 10 to 15 million more watch on television). How did college football get here? Here is a brief look at some of the game's most influential people and moments.

Walter Camp created many of the rules that are still part of the game today.

Walter Camp: Known as the "Father of American Football," the captain of the Yale football team in 1876 went on to put in place some of the biggest changes in the rules of the game. He reduced the number of players on each side to 11 and introduced the line of scrimmage.

NCAA: In 1906, the Intercollegiate Athletic Association of the United States was formed as a **governing body** for college football. That came about after a slew of football-related deaths—330 between the years of 1890 and 1905—caused leaders, including President Theodore Roosevelt, to wonder about the game's safety. Four years later, the name was changed to the National Collegiate Athletic Association, or NCAA.

Amos Alonzo Stagg: Another former Yale player, Stagg introduced many innovations in the game, including the huddle, uniform numbers, and the onside kick. He also won 314 games in a coaching career that spanned seven decades.

Rose Bowl: The "Granddaddy of Them All" was the first bowl game. The inaugural

Red Grange (see sidebar) was the first national football superstar while a collegian.

Rose Bowl was played on January 1, 1902, at Tournament Park in Pasadena. Michigan was leading Stanford 49–0 in the second half when the teams agreed to end the game with about eight minutes left. There are now 40 bowl games nationwide.

Knute Rockne: The **charismatic** coach who made Notre Dame as popular nationwide in the 1920s as baseball's New York Yankees. Rockne did not invent the forward pass but he popularized it, and he still owns the best winning percentage (.881, 105–12–5) in college football history.

Paul "Bear" Bryant: The patron saint of Alabama football, if not all of college football in the Deep South, the Bear led the Crimson Tide to six national championships and retired following the 1982 season with 323 career wins, the most in all of Division I at the time.

Red Grange

On October 18, 1924, Michigan played Illinois. Michigan had not lost in two seasons. That soon changed.

Michigan kicked off to Illinois back Harold "Red" Grange, who returned the ball 95 yards for a touchdown. In the next 12 minutes, Grange scored on runs of 67, 56, and 44 yards. Grange, known as "The Galloping Ghost," then scored on a 13-yard run. In the fourth quarter, he threw a touchdown pass as the Illini shocked Michigan 39–14.

Grange's effort was as momentous a performance as college football had ever witnessed. After the 1925 college season, he joined the NFL's Chicago Bears.

Alabama running back Derrick Henry hoisted the Heisman Trophy in 2015.

Heisman Trophy

The Heisman Trophy, which is awarded annually to college football's most outstanding player, is arguably the most famous trophy in all of sports. (Hockey fans might argue in favor of the Stanley Cup.) It is also a mess of contradictions.

The Heisman is presented in the heart of New York City, just off Times Square, which is about as far from the soul of college football as one can get. Second, while the award is presented to a player, it is named after a person who was better known as a coach (John W. Heisman), and that coach is best re-

Top 5 Heisman Trophy Busts in NFL history

membered for having been on the winning side of the most lopsided game in the sport's history (Georgia Tech 222, Cumberland 0, in 1916). Finally, the award honors an individual in the one sport, more than any other, in which teamwork is most vital.

The Heisman Trophy, voted on by hundreds of media members and past winners, has been presented annually by the Downtown Athletic Club since 1935. Only once has a player who primarily played defense won the award (Michigan defensive back Charles Woodson in 1997, who beat out quarterback Peyton Manning). The inaugural winner, Jay Berwanger of the University of Chicago, never pursued an NFL career. The model for the bust on the trophy was New York University player Ed Smith.

Boosters

Another thing that distinguishes college football from other sports is the rabid attention and support of boosters. What is a booster? Boosters are people, but they are also the money behind college football. Boosters are to college football what lobbyists or campaign contributors are to politicians.

Let's say that you happen to be a wealthy (make that, extremely wealthy) alumnus of a particular school. Maybe you did not even attend State U., but you are a passionate fan of its football team. You want to see the team do well. You want to help. There must be some way, you think, that your money would help the team win more games.

There is!

Boosters, who are officially recognized by the NCAA as "representatives of the university's athletic interests," are allowed to donate as much money to a school or, specifically, its athletic department—or, even more specifically, its football team—as they like. There is no limit, with one exception: None of the money may find its way into the players' pockets. It is against NCAA rules for schools, or their representatives, to pay players.

Nike founder and CEO Phil Knight is a proud alumnus of the University of Oregon. It's no coincidence that once Knight began donating huge sums of money to his alma mater, as well as helping the football team redesign its uniforms, that the Ducks went from an also-ran in the Pac-12 Conference to a perennial Top 10 powerhouse nationally. Just a few years ago, Knight donated $68 million to Oregon for a Football Performance Center. (In fairness to Knight, he has given lots of money for non-athletic ventures, too, such as $27 million for a library renovation.)

Thanks to Nike, Oregon's football team annually sports an array of colorful uniform designs.

Boosters are an essential source of revenue for major college football programs, but they potentially can be a problem, too. As soon

College football means marching bands, alumni support, great cheers, and classic rivalries.

as a booster is caught funneling money specifically to a player, or his family, the NCAA will impose harsh penalties.

From marching bands to behind-the-scenes boosters, college football is a unique experience off the field. For longtime fans and alumni, it's the continuation of a tradition going back decades. For students at the schools, it's a source of entertainment and community.

For players, it's a whole new ball game.

 # Text-Dependent Questions

1. What year was the first college football game played?

2. Name two of Walter Camp's innovations.

3. What do boosters do?

 # Research Project

Look up the all-time winners of the Heisman Trophy. What school has won the most? What positions have won the most often? What trends can you see during some periods of time?

CHAPTER 2

How many of these players in a 2015 college game will make it to the pros? Many think they have a shot, but few actually do.

PATHWAY TO THE PROS?

Almost every young man who accepts the offer of a scholarship to play college football dreams of playing in the NFL, but very, very few of those who dream of playing on Sundays ever do.

According to figures compiled by the NFL, fewer than 7 percent of the 310,000 high school seniors playing football each year will continue to play in college. Of that number, less than 2 percent of all the 15,000 or so college seniors playing football will find their names on an NFL **roster**. And for the 300 or so that do, the average length of an NFL career is less than three years.

Words to Understand

contiguous next to one another in a series

eligibility in this case, the right to continue to play on a college team, granted by both the school and the NCAA

roster the list of players on a sports team

understudy a term from the theater meaning a person waiting to take over a role in case the star (or, in sports, the starter) can't perform

Those are grim numbers for anyone who aspires to be the next Cam Newton. Simply playing at the collegiate level is both a demanding and rewarding experience. For the overwhelming majority of student-athletes who strap on shoulder pads and a helmet, the journey ends there.

Three (Four) Divisions

College football has three divisions: Division I, which is divided into two subdivisions; Division II; and Division III. The largest of these, Division I, comprises the Football Bowl Subdivision (FBS) and the Football Championship Subdivision (FCS). More than 90 percent of future NFL players compete at the Division I FBS and FCS levels.

Division II, which has about 150 programs, has far more players in the NFL than Division III. As of 2015 there were 120 D-II NFL players, among them running back Danny Woodhead and kicker Adam Vinatieri, each of whom have won Super Bowl rings.

Division III, whose schools generally have the smallest enrollments, has about 240 football programs.

On average, not even one D-III player per season makes an NFL roster. A rare example of success was former Mount Union wide receiver Pierre Garçon, who led the league in receptions in 2013 as a member of the Indianapolis Colts.

That's how the teams are arranged. What are the steps a player can go through in his college career? To succeed, he'll need a combination of timing, terminology, and technique.

Redshirting

Once a student enrolls at a school, he has five **contiguous** years to complete his four seasons of **eligibility**. On rare occasions, usually due to injury, the NCAA will grant a player a sixth year of eligibility.

The term redshirting means the practice of holding a player out for an entire season, most commonly during his freshman year, in order to delay the first year of his eligibility. From a coach's perspective, a player is more physically and emotionally developed in years two through five of his eligibility than he is in his first year. From a player's perspective, most freshmen are unlikely to see significant playing time, anyway, so why not use that first year to get used to college and to develop in the weight room?

A student exhausts a season of eligibility as soon as he participates in a game. Even if he only sees the field for one play the entire season, that year of eligibility is gone. The case when a freshman is first put into a game, particularly if it happens late in the season, is known as "burning his redshirt."

A player can be redshirted during any one of his first four seasons, but only once. If a player suffers a

College players spend as much time in the weight room as they do in the classroom…or, in some cases, more.

season-ending injury before playing in 20 percent of his team's games, he may be granted a medical hardship waiver, which works like a redshirt. The player does not lose that season of eligibility.

The Weight Room

In football, only kicking specialists and some quarterbacks can afford not to be physically superior. "Speed kills," as they say, and if speed is not your forte, then size and strength ought to be.

To that end, the strength coach is often the coach with whom players, particularly underclassmen, are most familiar. Thirty years ago, you could count the number of 300-pound (136-kg) players in the NFL on one hand. Today, at least four out of five starting offensive lineman at all of the premier FBS schools are 300-pounders. Evolution did not accelerate; training methods have.

Weight training, which incorporates weightlifting, cross-training, and a dedicated diet, has become a year-round pursuit in college football. How great an emphasis do college coaches place on strength train-

A closer look at college football training methods

ing? Scott Cochran, the strength coach at Alabama, the most successful college program of the past decade, earns approximately $500,000 per year. That's more than many Division I head coaches earn.

Off-Field Issues

College players spend three hours facing opponents in front of TV cameras and the fans. The rest of the week, they have to negotiate many other kinds of problems that can be even more dangerous than a stronger opponent. A college player can derail his dreams of an NFL career as easily off the field as he can on it.

For example, in January of 2015, De'Andre Johnson, a quarterback who had been named Florida's "Mr. Football" in 2014 at First Coast High School in Jacksonville, enrolled at Florida State. Johnson appeared to be a can't-miss prospect. Six months after Johnson enrolled, he found himself involved in a verbal altercation with a female student at a Tallahassee bar. The 19-year-old freshman struck the young woman in the face. Video cameras captured the incident. Seminoles coach Jimbo Fisher dismissed the talented player from the team "effective immediately." In an instant, a free college education and a possible ticket to the NFL vanished.

In the era of social media and near-omnipresent video cameras, where bad news can travel across the globe at the speed of a re-tweet, the behavior of a big-time college football player is almost on trial. Players need to understand that they are public figures; many are even celebrities. A poor decision off the field can be far more ruinous than a fumble or a dropped pass.

Transfer Time

Most positions in football rely on depth. Multiple players at the same position—for instance, defensive linemen or wide re-

Walk-Ons

At least 2,500 high school seniors are offered FBS scholarships each year. A few others succeed as "walk-ons."

When J.J. Watt graduated from high school, he hoped to play in his home state at the University of Wisconsin. The Badgers, however, did not offer him a scholarship. Watt accepted a scholarship to play at Central Michigan—but his heart was not in it. After one year, Watt transferred to Wisconsin without a scholarship. Technically, he was a "walk-on," and had to try out for the team. Two seasons later, Watt was the Badgers' MVP. He has become a three-time NFL defensive player of the year.

ceivers—earn playing time in a single game as coaches rotate them in and out.

Not so at the quarterback spot, where the starter rarely shares snaps with his backup.

At most schools, the position of quarterback is like being the leading man in a Broadway musical. No matter how large the cast, there can only be one. And if you happen to be the **understudy** for that lead role, you may find yourself highly frustrated. First-string quarterbacks get to sing solos; backup quarterbacks rarely even step out from behind the curtain.

Primarily for that reason, quarterbacks transfer to other schools more than players at any other position. In 2015, approximately 40 starting quarterbacks at the FBS level, including two of the four whose teams advanced to the four-team College Football Playoff—Jake Coker of Alabama and Baker Mayfield of Oklahoma—had begun their college careers elsewhere.

Any player is eligible to transfer schools, but the rate is just much higher among quarterbacks. If a player at the Division I FBS level transfers to another Division I FBS program, he must sit out one year before he may play again. That season is either the player's redshirt year or a lost season of eligibility.

The exception to that rule occurs if the player has graduated but still has one or more years of eligibility remaining. In that case, as happened with quarterback Russell Wilson (who played his final year at the University of Wisconsin in 2011 after graduating from North Carolina State), the transferred athlete may play immediately. Either way, the player still has five years in a row to complete his four seasons of eligibility.

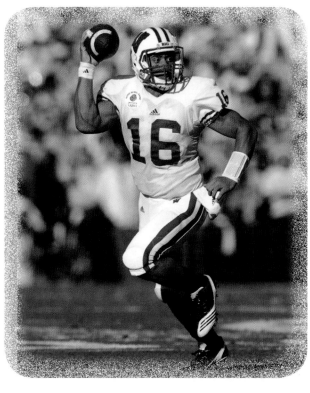

Russell Wilson used eligibility rules to play a year at Wisconsin even after graduating college.

Three and Out

The National Football League has a rule in place that states a prospective draftee must be three years removed from the date of his high school gradua-

tion before he is eligible to be drafted. The "three-year rule" has been challenged in the past, specifically by former Ohio State running back Maurice Clarett, who attempted to turn pro after his freshman season in 2002 in Columbus. Clarett's challenge went all the way to the Supreme Court, which upheld the NFL rule.

The tale of Maurice Clarett is a warning for players to keep other options open.

The NFL says that the rule is in place to protect young players. But while it does give players more time to develop physically and mentally, it also exposes them to risk. As a freshman running back at the University of South Carolina in 2010, Marcus Lattimore rushed for nearly 1,200 yards. In each of the following two seasons, he suffered injuries that required knee ligament surgery.

In the span of two years, Lattimore went from a certain first-round NFL pick to a fourth-round pick. He never played a down in the NFL.

For those select few who are certain first-round picks, the three-year rule poses a huge financial risk: Senior year is one more season that a player with the potential to play in the NFL, where the minimum salary is more than $400,000 per year, exposes himself to the risk of a career-ending injury.

Perks

While athlete-only dormitories were outlawed by the NCAA in 1996, every rule has a loophole. As long as a dorm has a general student population of at least 51 percent, a school may house an entire football team in one structure, and that building may be as plush as the school desires.

At the University of Oklahoma, Headington Hall is a residential palace. The $75 million edifice, which opened in 2013, houses 380 students. That means every Sooners player who wants to may reside there, though some upperclassmen live off campus.

Headington Hall has spacious rooms with individual bathrooms, a computer lab, game room, and even a movie theater.

"This place has everything," Sooners receiver Sterling Shepard said upon moving in. "What doesn't it have?"

Football players also have greater access to individual tutors—at bigger schools, a small army of tutors are fully dedicated to working solely with football players—and better meals. It is not a typical student experience.

Time Demands

The NCAA has a rule that says football players are allowed to spend a maximum of 20 hours per week in mandatory practice and competition. In reality, players spend at least double that amount of time on football.

While the rule is well intentioned—designed to remind both coaches and players, but primarily coaches, that these young men are college students—it has too many loopholes. Each week players may attend "voluntary" lifting sessions or position meetings, or they may "voluntarily" watch film of their opponent, or "voluntarily" study their playbooks or visit the training staff for medical treatment.

"The Twenty-Hour Rule doesn't work," says Big Ten commissioner Jim Delany. "The most important thing is there be a discussion about how prepared the student is, how the school accommodates prepared-ness, and how it all works."

Most colleges offer athletes from all sports extra help, such as tutors and study halls.

Despite the time demands, the typical gradua-tion rate for Division I football players is roughly 66 percent, which is slightly better than that of the ordinary student population. Some schools, such as Northwestern and Notre Dame, graduate an average of 97 percent of their players, which is fantastic. Others graduate less than 50 percent, which is troubling.

What can be mislead-ing about the graduation statis-tics is that the cross-section of majors is not representative of the

Can you be a college football player and graduate? Yes, but for more and more top stars, college is just a way to get to the NFL.

student body. Occasionally a top achieving player will major in engineering or be a pre-med, but those are the exceptions. At larger schools, players are often funneled into less demanding majors so that they will have a greater chance to succeed.

Overall, for college football players, the rewards are rare, the risks many, and the choices hard. They are provided with many opportunities to succeed, both on and off the field. They are also placed in front of temptations that can lead them off the path of success. The key to their success is to understand all the parts of the equation.

 Text-Dependent Questions

    1. How many years of eligibility does a college athlete have?

    2. What is a redshirt?

    3. What is a walk-on?

 Research Project

    From the past three NFL drafts, count how many players were chosen from FCS, Division II, and Division III schools. What were the percentages of each of the total number of players chosen?

CHAPTER 3

Thanks largely to TV money, schools can pay their head coaches, such as Alabama's Nick Saban, millions of dollars.

THE STATE OF THE GAME

In 2012, ESPN reached an agreement to televise annually the college football national championship game and its six associated bowls. The contract, which runs for 12 years through 2025, pays college football approximately $470 million per year.

That's a lot of money: Each FBS school gets more than $3.5 million per year, in addition to ticket sales, other television packages, and merchandise sales, etc. College football is an extremely **lucrative** business. Its bottom line is enhanced by the fact that the players are not paid salaries, but work in exchange for having their tuition paid, plus free room and board.

Words to Understand

amateurism playing a sport but not receiving any payments for doing so

lucrative high-paying

Do college football players have it better than most of their fellow students? In many ways, yes. They are able to graduate with no student debt, and have easy access to tutors, better meals, and free clothing. They are campus celebrities.

On the other hand, as the money involved in college football gets more and more absurd—a typical head coach at a major program is paid at least $3 million per year—it may seem less and less fair that the only people who are excluded from the bounty of revenue are the ones who are most responsible for its popularity: the players.

Is Anyone in Charge Here?

In college football, unlike the NFL, NBA, Major League Baseball (MLB), and the NHL, there is no commissioner. No one person or organization is actually in charge of the sport. The NCAA provides guidelines for **amateurism** and recruiting, but it does not provide referees, does not oversee bowl games or the playoff, and does not regulate scheduling.

No one is in charge in college football. That creates a certain amount of chaos. And many of the more powerful people in the sport prefer it that way.

Imagine a high school. It has a science department, an English department, a language department, and even an athletic department. All of these departments act in their own self-interest, but the school also has a principal. The job of the principal, among other roles, is to balance each department's interest against the overall welfare of the school.

Now imagine if the principal did not exist. That's college football.

The NFL Versus College

Let's compare college football to the NFL. Imagine if the Seattle Seahawks had to play their six NFC West divisional games, but then were allowed to play whomever they chose to play outside of those opponents. That's also college football.

Imagine if the Houston Texans decided that they no longer wanted to play in the AFC South but would prefer to play in the NFC North. And that the NFC North would welcome the Texans. If it were college football, the Texans would simply change divisions, after paying a fee.

The FBS is less a single, unified country than it is a loosely affiliated group of independent states. Those states are known as conferences. There are five major conferences in the FBS: the Atlantic Coast Conference (ACC), Big 12, Big Ten, Pacific-12 (Pac-12), and Southeastern (SEC). They are known as the "Power Five." There are also five minor conferences, which are known as the "Group of Five." Three schools—Army, BYU, and Notre Dame—do not belong to any conference and govern themselves.

Some fans enjoy the chaos and the lack of uniformity, while others do not. The Big 12 does not have a conference championship game (though it is considering adding one), while the other four

Power 5 conferences do. Notre Dame has all of its home games televised by NBC, an exclusive (and highly lucrative) deal that no other school enjoys. SEC schools rarely travel outside the South or play a non-conference game away from home, while others do.

The only even playing field in college football is the field itself. It's part of what makes the sports so intriguing, but also often so maddening, to outsiders.

Football is so big at Notre Dame that this mural is unofficially known as "Touchdown Jesus."

The Playoff

With all that confusion, one of the things that long has been most hotly debated by fans is how a single national champion is chosen. Several methods have been tried, but none perfectly . . . yet.

In 2014, the Football Bowl Subdivision (FBS) instituted a four-team playoff for the first time. Division II and Division III football, the lower divisions,

The Rose Bowl Game in Pasadena first was played in 1902.

have both staged multiple-team play-offs since 1973. In the FBS, however, for the longest time the season ended with a mix of bowl games, none of which were designated as a national-title contest. Extending back to shortly after World War II in the mid-1940s, conference champions were aligned with specific bowls. On New Year's Day in 1947, for example, the Rose Bowl began matching the champions of what are now the Big Ten and Pac-12 conferences. In that era, most often the two highest-ranked teams at the end of the season did not play one another in a bowl. The champions, instead, were chosen by a vote of sportswriters or coaches.

Then, in the 1998 season, the Bowl Championship Series (BCS) began. From that year until 2013, the top two teams, based upon a complex formula involving polls and computer rankings, met in one of four bowl games: the Rose, Fiesta, Sugar, or Orange. The sites rotated annually. The winner of that final game was clearly defined as the champion (though many continued to grumble about it).

Finally, in 2014, after years of fans and media griping about deserving teams being excluded from the process of deciding a national champion, the College Football Playoff was instituted. Each December, four teams are selected to compete in a single-elimination tournament by a 12-member selection committee.

Each year, the national championship game is played at one of six bowl sites: Cotton (Arlington, Tex.), Fiesta (Glendale, Ariz.), Orange (Miami Gardens, Fla.), Peach (Atlanta, Ga.), Rose (Pasadena, Calif.), or Sugar (New Orleans, La.). Two of the other six bowls act as the semifinal games. The bowl site that serves as the national championship game, however, does not substitute the title game for its bowl. It still plays its bowl on or about New Year's Day, then hosts the championship approximately 10 days later.

Conference Realignment

The Big 12 Conference has 10 member football schools, while the Big Ten has 14. Huh? Massachusetts, in New England, plays in the Mid-American Conference, while Colorado plays in the Pacific-12 Conference.

What is going on here? Conferences are no longer just made by geography. Adding more member schools means more money for the conferences, so several conferences now have unusual combinations of schools and cities. The process will continue, so fans should watch their schools' websites carefully for news of any changes.

In the first year of the play-off, the four schools chosen were, in order, Alabama, Oregon, Florida State, and Ohio State. Many fans and media members felt that the Buckeyes, who had lost to an unranked Virginia Tech team in September, did not belong in the playoff. But Ohio State, the final team selected, defeated Alabama, and then Oregon, to win the playoff. The College Football Playoff is in place through the 2025 season, so it remains to be seen if perfection has been reached.

Bowled Over

At the conclusion of the 2015 regular season, college football staged 40 bowl games. Eighty different schools, or nearly two-thirds of the programs in the 128-team FBS participated in bowls from Boise, Idaho, to the

Bahamas, and from Honolulu, Hawaii, to Yankee Stadium in New York. Bowls know no bounds.

In the not-too-distant past, bowls were perceived as a reward for an extraordinary season, not unlike a Christmas bonus. At the end of the 1990 season, there were 19 bowl games. In 2015, there were twice as many bowls, but certainly not twice as many outstanding teams. A dozen schools with 6–6 records accepted invitations to appear in bowl games. Three schools that lost more games than they won, all with 5–7 records, also appeared in bowls. You might say that college football has entered its participation-trophy era.

Why are there so many bowl games? Money and television. The largest bowls, such as the "New Year's Six" bowls, pay out more than $5 million per school. But the lesser bowl games, the so-

Michigan won the Buffalo Wild Wings Citrus Bowl, one of 40 bowl games played in the 2015 college season.

called "meaningless" bowls, pay less than $1 million per school. The Camellia Bowl, which was staged in Montgomery, Alabama, six days before Christmas, only paid out $100,000 per school to the two participants, Appalachian State and Ohio. That barely covers each team's meal expenses.

So, again, how come? The lesser bowls are exclusively televised by ESPN, which craves original programming over the Christmas holidays. Football games, even between mediocre opponents, draw far more viewers than other sports. The bowls themselves generate much of their revenue from their television rights deals with ESPN.

Hence, ESPN and the bowls themselves are profitable. The schools, which for the most part lose money by participating in smaller bowls, see it as a chance at national exposure. Kids like the idea of appearing on TV (who doesn't?), so it helps a coach with recruiting when he is able to tell a high school stud that his team went to a bowl last Christmas and appeared on ESPN.

The concept of bowls still has appeal, even if many bowls do not.

Uniforms Are Not Uniform

College football teams used to have two uniforms: home and away. The home team usually wore a jersey with its dominant color, and the visiting team wore white jerseys.

Then Oregon happened. The Oregon Ducks are the alma mater of Phil Knight, the founder of Nike, the revolutionary sportswear company that is based in Beaverton, Oregon. In the mid-1990s, Knight's team at Nike developed a brilliant scheme to attract the country's premier football talent to play in Eugene: Make the uniforms cooler.

Schools cannot pay their players, but there are other ways to appeal to them. Teenagers love looking good; Knight understood that better than most people. He did not just modernize the Ducks' uniforms, but his design team created different Ducks uniforms for almost every game. Different helmets, too.

As the Ducks became a national powerhouse in the 21st century, many programs that had been non-factors for decades followed suit (literally). Arizona State University never wears the same uniform, helmets including, more than once a season. Dozens of other programs, including traditional schools such as Notre Dame and Ohio State, wear alternate uniforms at least once a year. Why? Because players think it's cool, and you cannot win without players.

Who pays for all of this? The sportswear company (for example, Nike or Adidas or Under Armour) that has an exclusive deal with the school. But isn't there a rule against uniforms being, well, uniform? No. Remember when we said that nobody is in charge of college football?

For an enterprise that sees billions of dollars flow in and around it each year, college football remains a perplexing and confusing place, with no one truly in overall charge. Fans are often confused, while players sometimes take the biggest hits. But the game goes on, year after year.

Text-Dependent Questions

1. Why does the author say there are so many bowl games?

2. In what year did the current College Football Playoff start?

3. What company did Phil Knight start that made him the money he used to donate to Oregon?

 Research Project

This is more for fun than study: Look up a year of Oregon uniforms and pick your favorite. Then pick your favorite college team and design a few new uniform looks for them. Make sure to read about rules that govern safety for players—that is, how long pants need to be, size of shirts for shoulder pads, etc.

CHAPTER 4

Florida high school star Samuel Bruce wore his new school's colors when he announced on Signing Day 2015 that he was going to the University of Miami.

RECRUITING

For an ever-growing number of fans, the first day of college football season does not include tailgating, or marching bands, or even a game. It does not even occur in early September.

For a school's most enthusiastic and passionate fans, the first day of the season falls on the first Wednesday of February. That date, as these lovers of the game know, is National Signing Day. It is the first day that high school seniors may formally commit to a specific school by signing a National Letter of Intent, or NLI.

It is often said that recruiting is the **lifeblood** of every college football program. That is true. The best coaches always seem to have the best players. In fact, at least half of the job in college coaching is recruiting. Even the brightest coach needs talented players in order to win.

Words to Understand

ambivalent unable to decide, not committed to one course of action

leverage the ability to direct the course of action in a decision

lifeblood most important ingredient

verbally in a spoken, as opposed to written, way

No Draft

In the National Football League, teams acquire talent from the college level each spring via a draft. Teams select college seniors—as well as a small number of juniors who have declared for the draft and forfeited their final season of eligibility—in reverse order of how well they finished the previous season. For example, the team with the league's worst record selects first, while the team that won the Super Bowl picks last, unless there are trades of draft picks.

In the NFL, the teams hold total control as to where college players begin their careers. In college, the exact opposite occurs. Incoming college players (high school seniors) are free to choose at which school they will play. Of course, the more talented the player, the more choices and the greater **leverage** that player has.

Many times, those players, or student-athletes, are offered full scholarships in return for their services. The better the player is, the more scholarships he will be offered. It's a little bit like finding a date for senior prom.

In any one academic year, an FBS school is allowed to sign no more than 25 incoming players to scholarships. The maximum number of players on scholarship for the entire roster is 85.

Behind the scenes of college football recruiting

You are good enough at math to know that 25 times 4 equals more than 85. Every year, a team loses players, either because they transfer, or suffer career-ending injuries, or simply choose to no longer play. But at any one point, a school can have no more than 85 players on scholarship.

Two more items about scholarships: Most fans think they are four-year scholarships, but they are actually one-year contracts that both parties must renew each year. Schools very rarely pull a scholarship from a player after he has played a year or two for them. To do so would look bad to future recruits.

Also, when high school players sign their NLI, they must send that document to the school. Players sign the NLI, then fax it into the school. Email is not accepted. Nor is texting. Some things change more slowly than others.

Never-Ending Cycle

There is never a day off in recruiting. Most coaching staffs have a recruiting coordinator, which is a full-time job. Position coaches are usually assigned geographic areas in which to recruit. Never a day goes by when a coach will not email or phone at least one player, if not most of the top players, in his assigned area. A player may have even already **verbally** committed to that school, but the coach will still phone or write him.

Recruiting players is like courting a prospective spouse or girlfriend. You can always do more to let them know how much you care. The key thing to remember is that it is all about access: coaching staffs seek as much contact as possible with a potential player (known as a signee or a prospect), so the NCAA uses restrictions in order to keep a certain level of sanity—although it still can be rather insane.

National Signing Day—always the first Wednesday in February—marks the end of the year's recruiting cycle. Then the process starts all over again.

The Calendar

Let's take a trip around one entire recruiting year, using 2015 as our example.

February 4: National Signing Day. First day a high school senior may sign his NLI.

February 6–April 14: Quiet Period. During a quiet period, coaches and potential signees are forbidden from any type of off-campus contact. A player may, and is often encouraged to, visit campus to get an idea of what the school is like. Electronic contact such as emails and/or phone calls are permitted.

April 15–May 31: Evaluation Period. Coaches may visit a prospect's school and assess him athletically and/or academically. The coach may talk to the prospect's coaches, teachers, and school administrators, but may have no direct contact with the player himself other than to say hello. Prospects may visit the school. Electronic contact is permitted.

June 1–June 26: Quiet Period.

June 27–July 10: Dead Period. No in-person contact is permitted, anywhere. Electronic contact is permitted. This, not coincidentally, is when most college coaches go on vacation.

July 11–November 28: Quiet Period. However…

September 1–November 30 is an Evaluation Period. Schools have a maximum of 42 select dates to visit prospective schools. This is also when prospects make official visits. (More on that below.)

December 1–December 13: Contact Period. Coaches may visit with players and their families anywhere, regardless of location. This is also a two-week period during which coaches put on weight, because no one wants to insult mama's home cooking. This is one of two hard-sell periods for coaches.

December 14–January 13: Dead Period.

January 14–January 30: Contact Period again.

January 31: Quiet Period.

February 1–Signing Day: Dead Period.

Official and Unofficial Visits

As soon as a prospect completes his first day of classes of his senior year of high school, he is allowed to take an official visit to a college campus. A prospect is allowed to take a maximum of five official visits, and each visit may last no more than 48 hours.

Official visits are when coaches try to really sell a prospect on their school. The school pays for the student's transportation, lodging, and all of his expenses. It also does its best to give that senior a truly memorable experience. An official visit usually coincides with a big home football game weekend. The prospect stays in dorms, meets with players and teachers and alumni, and often attends special events.

A student is allowed to take as many unofficial visits as he likes as well. The school does not pay for this, but may provide the student with a few free tickets to a sporting event.

Recruiting Websites

Twenty-five years ago, a few individuals provided recruiting services, selling publications that rabid college football fans could send away for through the mail. Both the men who provided those services and many of the fans who paid for them were thought to be, well, a little too passionate.

That has changed. Recruiting is its own industry now, with dedicated sites such as Rivals.com and Scout.com having large, obsessed fan bases. Those and other sites rank the top 250–300 high school seniors and juniors. They rank players by position, and rank schools in terms of how well they're recruiting.

Recruiting websites have helped create an entirely new way of speaking about players. Players are not only ranked numerically, but they are also allotted anywhere from two to five stars, with five being the best.

Penn State coach James Franklin worked the phones until the last minute, trying to recruit players to his team.

Solid Verbal

Have you ever been invited to a birthday party or an overnight camping trip and thought to yourself, "I'll go if my friend goes?" Verbal commitments in college football are a lot like that.

A verbal commitment, that is, a player promising to sign an NLI with a school, is not binding to either party. Either side may break its commitment right up until the player puts pen to paper and signs his name on the NLI. However, if a school "pulls" a scholarship from a player, it is bad for its reputation. Players often "de-commit" from their verbal agreements; while schools don't like it, that's life when dealing with **ambivalent** teenagers.

Schools begin making scholarship offers in earnest to players during the spring of their junior years. The feeling among coaching staffs is that if they can get a four- or five-star athlete to verbally commit early, his presence will help persuade other players to sign with that class. Also, there are no restrictions to that verbally committed five-star player from recruiting other prospective teammates.

The verbal commitment helps coaches get an understanding not only of whom they have rounded up, but also whom they should stop trying to recruit.

Not that some schools won't quit attempting to lure a player who is verbally committed elsewhere to their campus. All's fair in love and war…and recruiting.

Camps

Coaches are not allowed to contact players until September 1 of their junior year of high school. Coaching staffs are eager to get acquainted with elite players long before their junior years, though, and players are eager to learn more about potential schools and coaches.

The solution? Summer camps, which may last anywhere from one session to an entire week. The on-campus football camp, which the player must pay for, provides a chance for coaching staffs and fresh-man and sophomore players to get acquainted. At Stanford University, the David Shaw football camps cost $200 for a full day or $350 overnight. The University of Notre Dame offers camps ranging from one day to four, with the top price being $525.

It's an arrangement that helps both sides. While a young football player is being provided with elite-level instruction, it is also an opportunity for him to showcase his talent in front of coaches. The coaching staffs are also evaluating more than just a player's physical gifts; they are assessing his maturity and how well he responds to instruction.

However, reflecting the role camps play in recruiting, in 2016, the NCAA banned coaches from having such camps anywhere but their own campus. Until the rule change, "satellite" camps were a way to meet recruits in action around the country.

From the moment a high school player catches the eye of college coaches, he is the target of an onslaught of recruiting. Yes, it is very regulated and some schools do bend or break the rules, but the process winds up with most players getting a scholarship somewhere.

From that point, they join the business of big-time college football, with all the good and bad things that go with it. Thousands of young men get the chance at a free college education, a chance they might never have had. Some will take full advantage, but others will be taken advantage of. As with anything relating to school, the best solution is study—whether that is studying in the classroom, or studying the process of recruiting and being a college football player.

In the end, in most cases, the hard work pays off one way or another.

 # Text-Dependent Questions

1. What is an NLI?
2. What is an official visit?
3. What is a verbal commitment?

 # Research Project

Check out some of the recruiting websites. See if any students at your school or in your area are highly ranked. If you have any local heroes, try to interview them about the process of recruiting that they are going through. What have they learned about it? What has been the most surprising or hardest part? What factors will go into their final decision?

Find Out More

Books

Benedict, Jeff and Armen Keteyian. *The System: The Glory and Scandal of Big-Time College Football*. New York: Anchor Books, 2014.

Editors of Sports Illustrated. *Sports Illustrated: The College Football Book*. New York: Sports Illustrated, 2008.

Whittingham, Richard. *Rites of Autumn: The Story of College Football*. New York: The Free Press, 2001.

Websites

www.ncaa.com/sports/football
The NCAA's official site features all the latest news, plus lots of video highlights.

www.sports-reference.com/cfb/
If you're looking for facts and figures about college football history, this member of the sports reference family of websites is the place to go.

SERIES GLOSSARY OF KEY TERMS

alma mater the school that someone attended

analytics in sports, using and evaluating data beyond traditional game statistics to predict a player's future success

brass a slang term for the high-ranking executives of an organization

bundling in television, the concept of customers paying for a set of cable channels with one set fee

bye weeks the weeks that NFL teams do not play a game; each team gets one bye week per season

credentialed provided with an official pass allowing entry into a private or restricted area

eligibility in this case, the right to continue to play on a college team, granted by both the school and the NCAA

endorsement support and praise offered by a paid spokesperson for a product or service

expansion team a new franchise that starts from scratch

feedback information used to improve something

general managers members of a sports team's front office in charge of building that club's roster

leverage the ability to direct the course of action in a decision

merger to combine into one

perennial occurring or returning every year; annually

protocol in this instance, a pre-planned series of steps or tests undertaken by medical professionals working with players

public relations the process of telling the public about a product, service, or event from the "company" point of view

red zone for the team with possession of the football, the area of the field from the opponents' 20-yard line to the goal line

special teams the kicking game in football: kickoffs, punts, field goals, and extra points

traumatic in medicine, describing an injury that is very significant, resulting in damage to body tissues

INDEX

CREDITS

(Dreamstime.com: DT) Harpers Weekly 6; Ruth Peterkin/DT; Billy Hathorn/Wiki from Natl Port Gall 11; Rich Graessle/Icon Sportswire/Newscom 14; Joshua Rainey/DT 17; Gerald Mothes/DT 18; Aspenphoto/DT 20; Jerry Coli/DT 23; Steven Pepple/DT 24; Chris Williams/Icon SMI/Newscom 29; Phil Masturzo/KRT/Newscom 30; Tyler Olson/DT 33; Michael Zhang/DT 34; Jon Soohoo/UPI/Newscom 36; Ric Tapia/Icon Sportswire/Newscom 38; Susan Sheldon/DT 41; Nicholas Burningham/DT 42; David Rosenblum/Icon Sportwire/Newscom 45; Charles Trainor Jr./TNS/Newscom 50; Nabil K. Mark/MCT/Newscom 57.

ABOUT THE AUTHOR

John Walters is the senior sportswriter at *Newsweek*. Walters was a full-time staffer at *Sports Illustrated* from 1989 to 2001, and 2003 to 2006. He graduated from the University of Notre Dame in 1988 and has written a book about the school's football history titled, *Notre Dame: Golden Moments*. He has won two Sports Emmys and resides in New York City.